Fear and Promise

Kirk House Publishers

Fear and Promise

REMEMBERING THE YEAR 2020

Evelyn Klein (signature)

EVELYN D. KLEIN

Fear and Promise: Remembering the Year 2020
Copyright © 2022 by Evelyn D. Klein.

All rights reserved. No part of this book may be used or reproduced in any manner whatsoever without written permission of the author except in the case of brief quotations embodied in critical articles and reviews.

The information in this book is distributed as an "as is" basis, without warranty. Although every precaution has been taken in the preparation of this work, neither the author nor the publisher shall have any liability to any person or entity with respect to any loss or damage caused or alleged to be caused directly or indirectly by the information contained in this book.

First Edition
Paperback ISBN: 978-1-952976-40-7
eBook ISBN: 978-1-952976-41-4
Hardcover ISBN: 978-1-952976-42-1
Library of Congress Control Number: 2022903636

Cover and Interior Design by Ann Aubitz based on a drawing by Evelyn D. Klein
Illustrations by Evelyn D. Klein

Published by Kirk House Publishers
1250 E 115th Street
Burnsville, MN 55337
Kirkhousepublishers.com
612-781-2815

Acknowledgments

Grateful acknowledgment is made to previous publications of the following poems:

"When in Lockdown," "Nine Pandemic Ways of Thinking:" reading at AAUW, Saint Paul, 2021.

"Quarantine Companions," Ramsey County Library anthology: *This Was 2020*, 2021.

"Inspiration," 2020, "Nine Pandemic Ways of Thinking," 2021: *The Minnesota Scholar*.

For my children,
for the history buffs
and observers among us
and to the creative spirit
that flows and flows
a river of seeing, hearing,
feeling, thinking, and speaking,
always creating
in isolation or in a crowd,
in light and in darkness,
over smooth riverbed
or rocky terrain,
around obstructions,
and through crevices,
a river that flows steadily
to the gulf of delivery
in times of fear and promise alike.

Introduction

As we watched the news of the Corona virus outbreak in Wuhan, China, in 2019 on TV, many of us were in disbelief of what we saw, the spread of the virus, its intensity, the number of hospitalizations and deaths, followed by makeshift hospitals and morgues to accommodate the overflow of patients. And we saw, subsequently, strictly enforced mandates for the wearing of masks, quarantines, and social isolation.

It was not something we could imagine, then, happening in America. Had we not stayed safe from the Ebola outbreak in Africa in recent years? Did we not manage to curtail the spread of HIV in our own country before that? But when the Corona virus first appeared in America, it reminded some people of the polio outbreak in the mid-20th century with its life-altering effects. And historians pointed to the Spanish flu of 1918 that wiped out so many lives, the last such serious viral invasion of mega proportions to affect the country. The Corona virus, it was said, was an enemy that had to be defeated.

One of my independent scholar cohorts said that someone should keep track of the Covid-19 pandemic for posterity. That inspired me to write a poetic version, including the many challenging events of an entire year, framed in the pandemic, a year like no other.

For me, writer, observer isolated as all of us were, the year's challenges quickly led to a pressing task to carry on a conversation of great urgency, though with pen and paper. Question was not only how to survive the pandemic itself but also how to cope with the changes it invoked, address the racism that surfaced, and deal with the realities and unrealities of an election taking place in an arena that moved between the real and virtual, the personal and the official, all the while seeking to separate truth from fiction, stay safe, and survive holding on to one's own equilibrium, often sending me, like so many, to the natural world for sanctuary, refuge, and reprieve.

It seemed that poetry would be a particularly suitable conveyance for setting forth such a discourse and chronicle, poetry with its spontaneity, compactness, and figurative language to take readers there as spectators and leave them to their own conclusions as they read *Fear and Promise, Remembering 2020*.

~Evelyn D. Klein

Contents

I. In the Beginning: Alone

The Beginning	2
Waiting	4
Lockdown	6
Wear a Mask	8
Who Would Have Thought	10
Crossing	12
Night	13
Easter Visit	14
Road Ahead	16
April Day	17
Alone – Together	18
Stay at Home	19
Social Distancing	21
The Moon	23
Sheltering in Place	24
Connection	25
When in Lockdown	27
Graduation Sendoff 2020	28
We Are in this Together	29
May Birthday	31
Eye on the World	33

II. Pandemic, Wildfires and Demonstrations: Let's Get through this Together

A Second Look	36
Death and Demonstrations	38
Season of Construction,	41
They Tell Us	43

What is Forever?	44
Overshadowed	47
Zooming In	48
Moving Forward in a Pandemic	50
4th of July	52
Creation	54
Our Creation	55
Between Worlds	57
A Piece of the Pie	59
Light Within	61
Legacy	63
Seesaw	65
Keeping Calm	67
Sundays	69
Mondays	71
Tuesday	73
Kitchen Table	74

III. Pandemic Campaign: At a Distance

Freedom and Opportunity	76
California Burning	78
Summer's End	80
Top of the Hill	82
The House Across the Way	83
School Is Back in Session	85
Photo Shoot	87
Wildfires on the West Coast	89
Wildfires Moving North	91
The Chase	92
Waiting for Change	94
Construction Season Ending	96
The Neighbor	98
Changing Season	99
October Day	102
Reconnect	104

Vote for Your Life	106
A Rushing of Clouds	108
Native Peoples Day	110
Cloud Watching	112
Old Friends	113
Pandemic Fatigue	115
Gone Virtual	117
Moving Forward	118

IV. From Elections through Holidays: Staying Safe

Haunted	122
The Discourse	124
Birthday Shopping	126
Fall Campaign	128
Halloween Ghosts	130
Geraniums	132
Roses and Books	133
Autumn's Hub	135
Moving On	137
November Maneuvers	139
Thanksgiving 2020	141
Black Friday	143
A Gathering	144
Inspiration	145
Nine Pandemic Ways of Thinking	146
The Train of 2020	147
Advent reflections	149
Christmas Eve Light	150
Christmas Day	152
Year's End	154
Promise	156
Quarantine Companions	157

Section I
In the Beginning: Alone

The Beginning

2020 begins in ordinary ways.
January's sunshine, increasing daylight
spur us on like African violets sending blossoms
in early anticipation of spring.

Reports from Wuhan and a new virus spreading
dominate news. Soon temporary
emergency centers spring up there
like mushrooms. And we wonder
about reports of rising cases.

Concern grows in the U.S., yet
danger seems remote,
the way it was with other viruses
emanating in far-away places, remote
as China itself and its politics.

But when the first case is detected
in the state of Washington in late January,
it catches our attention. Cases spreading
through European states bring the reality home –
a pandemic, invisible enemy is steadily advancing.

The U.S. is not exempt from or immune to this spread.
Reports of source and quarantine for travelers,
isolation for populations let us know it is serious.
Large gatherings are discouraged, until
they are closed altogether with emergency measures
suggested by healthcare experts,

mandated by governors.

We leave our usual gatherings disconcerted,
wondering if we were exposed.
The world we know and frequent,
places where we shop, friends we visit,
family we regularly see, all except for essentials,
moved off into the distance. Life has morphed
into a science fiction deserted landscape. Only
African violets driving blossoms
and other houseplants offer continuity now

Waiting

Late March sun lights sky,
warms air.
Melted snow leaves tall grass
thatched, straw-like.
Lake's center still harbors ice
which breaks up here and there.

On lake's west side,
where water gently pulsates,
geese line up on shore's edge,
leisurely, side by side, grooming,
resting in their grassy sanctuary.

I stop and watch them,
where the path runs closer to the lake,
engrossed, surprised, lingering,
having escaped from daily isolation.
How long this pandemic?

On lake's east side,
near shore's open waters,
two trumpeter swans swim
in company of ducks.

Birds returning,
lining lake on both shores,
offer comfort, continuity
on an unpredictable journey
at a time of social distance.

We all now walk the path
around the lake silently,
without "Hi!" or smile
in a seeming rush
to an obscure destination,
while nature holds its steady course.

Lockdown

Days devoid of people,
siege brought us inside.
We survey spring cleaning,
sort out activities and involvements
for Easter ahead.

We walk in the wilderness
of social distance,
become islands in the sun,
where writing extends
breath of life.

The trip to the grocery store
takes us through once lively streets
now a ghost town of closed businesses.
This remains our sole weekly odyssey
into a world, where an invisible foe lingers,
ready to ambush, God knows when.

Safe at home, we turn to the phone,
check in with family,
seek out neglected friends,
nearly forgotten relatives,
sometimes renewing old bonds,
sometimes chatting awkwardly.

The notion to write hovers,
as I seek to finalize submission
of a linguistics manuscript

but hold back to add
more words of unbelief
than I could ever have imagined,

as if that would set the world
that is out of whack and out of touch
on its axis again.

Wear a Mask

Like from a babe in the woods,
word comes down the voice of denial,
"It's just like the flu."

Like mice seeking shelter in fall,
health care workers scramble
to prepare for the onslaught of illness, scramble
for needed equipment evading their domain,
leaving them short, while manufacturers scramble
to meet evolving need.

Then the word is out: "Wear a mask."
Make your own. Any covering for nose and mouth
will do. It's not for a masked ball or
incognito appearance, nor infringement of rights,
just a commonsense health measure.

With stores closed, I scavenge in the garage,
scavenge through boxes of old fabrics
from a long-discarded time in life, when sewing
told my story. Where is that cotton fabric now?

In the closet, I find an old, white
cotton tablecloth, mended here and there,
handed down from my mother, just right
for face masks for family and friends.

Soon, the effort takes me back to past days of sewing
and the discovery that it takes longer to rip out

wrong seams than it does to stitch them together.
Old routine gradually returning, I am now stitching away
on a wardrobe of masks for my daughter and me,
for starters, as I wonder,
where are we headed with this?

Who Would Have Thought?

Who would have thought,
news of the Corona virus
would spread more than words west?
The public was told not to worry;
it will soon pass.

Who would have thought
masks and lockdowns
would spread around the globe?
People were told
it was all a conspiracy.

Who would have thought
businesses would freeze,
as hospitals are overrun by Covid-19 patients?
"We need to flatten the curve,"
health experts warn.

Who would have thought
people would lose their jobs
through no fault of their own?
They are waiting for a stimulus package
from their government.

Who would have thought
empty streets and empty grocery store shelves,
reminiscent of times of war,
would become order of the day,
sparking fear?

The virus called Corona,
renamed Covid-19, arrives just when
longed-for spring was about to begin.
But summer will soon remedy the plight,
people are given to believe.

Crossing

This house sails
on waves of pandemic
to an uncertain destination,
a vessel on the ocean of time.

The ship, flanked
by distant, untouchable life,
accompanied
by speculations of the journey ahead
to a land of the unknown,
holds a steady course.

The ocean's curve
to the horizon
displays clouds gathering
above trees on a distant
island for which this ship
sets course to wait out the storm.

How far to the nearest harbor?
How long the voyage?

Night

Night gently descends
raspberry wings of setting sun,
while super moon gains
prominence over frozen lake,
signs heavenly bodies
still hold their course.

Night moves us inside.
Nightly routine holds us steady,
leads to musings and plans,
letting us forget
climate change and economy,
election and virus.
For now.

We find ourselves
traveling in presence of crowds.
They speak to me
in distant, grey dreams.
Once awake,
I forget what they were about.

How long to sunrise?

Easter Visit

April's warmer days invite
long or short walks,
alone – together in the park.

Then winter's last breath
blows in six inches of snow,
but I'm not dreaming
of a white Easter.

Churches hold virtual services,
preaching to empty pews,
to anyone who cares to watch,
listen. Some send off their flock
with drive-by Easter blessings.

My daughter calls to set up
a family gathering via Skype,
but Skype appears reluctant
to accept the information
in this game of hide and seek.

At last, mother, daughter, son
visit virtually in this new kind
of Easter celebration,
while treats wait in my cupboard
and surprise gift rests in their closet.

From one to the other,
we pass conversation

of activities, plans for the week,
delivered face to face,
framed by our own space
for revival of our spirits.

We part with virtual hugs and kisses,
my daughter beaming off,
having managed to bring us together
in holy grace of family reunion.

How high the number of cases?
"Still rising," news accounts state.

Road Ahead

The white La Crosse knows
the way with me
behind the wheel.

A pleasant spring day invites,
except for ominous dark clouds
billowing distantly
on the horizon.

Ahead, the road is light,
partly sunny.
I forge on, full speed,
confident there is time
to beat the weather,
until the road comes
to a sudden abyss, oh –
bathed in springtime light
as far as the eye can see,
below and ahead.

I awaken suspended
to the day,
having seen those distant,
ominous clouds
in dreams
weeks before.

April Day

At the window,
African violets blossom
shades of red, blue, pink,
purple, and white
in April's glory,
soothing troubled times.

Outside,
crabapple and spruce stir
in crisp wind,
spirits undisturbed
by pandemic.
Two finches,
one male the, other female, dart
between trees and white fence,
warbling life's love affair.

Alone – Together

Church was empty in the dream
devoid of pews, altar, furnishings.
In front,
domed ceiling,
two large stained-glass windows
let in bright light:

The church was packed
with silent grey figures,
like those in a comic book,
standing motionless side by side.
None looked familiar.

I found myself standing
in front, facing the crowd
where the minister normally stands,
next to some wiring
like a mike
but without sound:

How would I address
this audience
in this peculiar setting?
What could I say
that they would want to hear?

Stay at Home

Stay at home
is not a new lifestyle
for those who work from home.
But when all the world
temporarily
disappears inside,
streets turn ghost town,
returning the out-of-doors
to wild creatures.
When making face masks
is no longer enough,
when resources usually found
at the grocery store threaten
with empty shelves,
we pray: "Give us this day
our daily bread…"

Then baking carries me forward.
A recipe so elusive in the past
now finds its way,
with the familiar dough
I so carefully mix
with basic ingredients, energy of love,
adding mashed fruit, flavorings, and sugar
that hold the relationship.
All that's required now is
to add walnuts, mix with dedication and care,
fold dough of affection
into the pan of continuity,

remembering to keep the oven on
for the required time
for a banana bread sure to reunite
a "socially distant" family.

Social Distancing

Social distance
        startles.
At grocery store, drug store
        it safeguards.
In the park on the path,
        it hardly exists.
When adult children visit,
        it jars.
Then long phone conversations
        with family and friends
reconnect.

Zoom and Skype replace meetings
        like side shows,
bringing us, virtually,
        into each other's homes,
celebrity and ordinary folk
        alike.

Distance learning
        challenges students and parents,
exposing the many sides
        of teaching, learning, parenting.

On the balcony,
        people sing.
On the driveway,
        they draw pictures.
On the street,

   some wear costumes.

Food banks hand out
   groceries and meals.
Some businesses and restaurants serve
   curbside customers.
Some churches bestow
   curbside blessings.

A small crowd gathers
   at governor's mansion
with signs and outcries:
"Open Minnesota."
   (but "You can't please all the people
all the time," Lincoln once said.)
   Yet meat packing plants close
with rising cases,
   redirect and partially reopen,
while cases and death tolls
   climb.

How high, did you say?

The Moon

From the study window,
early in the evening,
I see full moon cast its light
over rooftops,
brighter than the lanterns,
diverting attention from my task,
leaving me to gasp in awe.

When the moon comes
to the bedroom window
later that night,
it casts a shadow of the spruce tree
the whistling wind makes dance across the blinds,
drawing my attention momentarily,
leaving me to gasp in awe.

Sheltering in Place

Sheltering in place
in view of rising Corona cases,
each household,
singles, families, friends,
live on their own island,
near a sea of people
in the storm of pandemic.

We see others only
from a distance, on Skype or Zoom
untouchable as in a dream,
visit grocery or pharmacy
as if in shark infested waters.

We think the surge
will soon ebb down,
only to be told,
the next wave may soon rise
where it began.

Meanwhile, forces that be
ease restrictions,
anticipate re-opening economy,
returning to election rallies,
while cases spread.

How deep the water, honey?

Connection

We would talk on the phone
every Sunday evening
to share stories of our busy lives.
As more doors to social interactions close,
including monthly family dinners,
my son adds a mid-week call,
just to make sure we stay well connected.

It's become more than a keeping in touch:
it's become a rolling out, a sharing
of our daily activities and thoughts,
wishes and hopes,
frustrations and accomplishments,
no matter how seemingly small or
acutely significant.

      He always approached life creatively,
inquisitively, from the time he
was a toddler, fascinated by toy cars,
carrying it forward as elementary schooler,
drawing souped up cars, that now decorate my wall,
as high schooler, refurbishing his first car,
before he was even old enough to drive.
And the boy who sat in the rocking chair
sometimes writing stories on his lap,
forged his dreams,
into life's automotive passion
on racetracks of technology.

Now we carry on our talks from pandemic
to politics to computers and cars and more,
not so much mother to son or son to mother
but more like two trusting adults, good friends
who have known each other for a long time.

When in Lockdown

Where can she go
in a lockdown
but outdoors
to the grounds,
where she lives

My daughter collects trash
in a plastic bag,
cleans up the world
beset by pandemic.

She decides to clear weeds
around cluster of trees and shrubs,
until she aches
and strains to stand up straight.

The young woman wants nature to thrive
that she can enjoy,
from her window,
goings on of robins and chickadees.

In springtime's flurry, flocks
of birds have long since disbanded
in pairs with tasks of nesting.
after their long journey.

It's worth the aching muscles
to see life run its normal course outdoors,
while working the body
tired of confinement.

Graduation Sendoff 2020

Yesterday lies behind you.
Today offers a springboard.
Tomorrow forges a new existence,
where change paves the road
and success builds on dreams and chance.
May your road take you far.
Go Graduates, go!

We Are in this Together

They arrive, each in his and her own car,
use the open garage
to stash their Easter-egg-like surprise
with gifts like cards and flowers and such
to be surveyed at a distance.

The main event still awaits,
where we break the cycle
of round-table dinner in exchange
for round-the-lake salute to Mother's Day.
Lockdown has made the heart ache.
Today we celebrate with mask
and social distance,
for we know who we are,
walk a triangle down the street
to the path that lets us forget,
for the moment, our anonymity.

The path fills our cup of humanity
as we trudge around the lake,
satiating our hunger for togetherness.
I reintroduce my adult children
to trees which I drew, which since have changed,
when my daughter spots heron
near shore across the lake
and pair of ducks right near us.
On muddy shoreline waters, we consider
small mounds, work of muskrats,
as my son points out, because beavers

would have felled all the trees nearby.

Having shared in nature of mutual spirit,
we return to courtyard of our start
talk of past dinners, new recipes,
and upcoming celebrations,
listening to the music of each other's voices.
In distant triangle of our gestured embrace,
we then part.

May Birthday

Family celebration of dinners
become life celebrations of nature walks
during "social distancing."
Chats consider
changing trees and bird life,
our unfolding lives,
evolving neighborhood,
people moving in and out,
the city's project
of a storm filtration system
laid across the open meadow
behind town homes,
to homeowners' surprise and chagrin.

Celebration turns
to red geranium planter
son and daughter present to me,
brightening invisible smiles.
For what is a celebration
without flowers,
and personalized greeting cards,
pedals of affection.
After the walk,
we sit in the courtyard,
while my daughter serves
three separate mini cakes,
one for each,
autonomous as our individual lives.
On the one lettered "Happy birthday,"

she lights three candles.
"We're not counting years today,"
her smiling eyes underline,
"only wishes," she adds.
Three unspoken wishes: staying safe,
supporting each other,
cherishing our connection,
blown, like seeds, into spring winds,
will do fine.

Eye on the World

In the absence of social presence,
television has become company,
steady eye on the world,
moving closer into our daily lives,
in a personal way –
It is music of background voices,
entertainer and messenger,
a filling empty space of our days
with "virtual" life
in this new way of living.

TV draws us into its spell,
from its platform of mythological powers
for better or worse,
in truth, make-believe, or lies,
joy or pain or simple diversion
with voices we hear,
know like our own best friends but
that do not hear or see, or know us,
but whom we follow, mesmerized, until
we forget our every-day tasks at hand
absorbed in our separate, listless days.

This one-eyed messenger,
on wings of electronics,
sweeps into our newly encapsuled lives
reminiscent of Orwell's 1984. It promises
to be our community, our state,
our country, even our world –

our new, extended neighbors, our cause.
We hold on tight not to miss the latest nuance
of all that takes place in that outside world.
Because all has become personal that once
was impersonal, remote – the political, the economic,
the educational, the medical, the systemic –
the struggle, the sacrifice, the tragedy, the hope,
because all the people truly matter,
because they are parts of one body,
the one family of humanity.

Section II
Pandemic, Wildfires, Death, and Demonstrations: Let's Get through this Together

A Second Look

We watch the world on-screen
in living color, words, and actions
like witnesses to actual events
but in a one-eyed point of view
without peripheral vision.

We see our personal world
from our own one-eyed perspective,
set by our turf and talents,
move forward on one-way tracks
without depth perception.

Left with pieces of so many puzzles,
I sift through what I hear,
sort through what I see,
sift and sort the meaning of it all,
sift and sort, sift and sort
in a merry-go-round of thoughts.

For what I hear and see
may only constitute fractions of the whole,
composed of truths, half truths,
or outright lies that need examining
time and again,

leaving me to ponder
in woods and underbrush of thought,
to find the way to the whole.
And I write my way through life's landscape,

its novel variations,
challenges and contradictions,
disappointments and successes
into open country of reality,
seeking truth revealed, penned
from internal perspective
as if looking for the holy Grail
but wanting to make sense of it all.

Death and Demonstrations

Last week of May
people deal with a pandemic
that steadily advances, disjoints
their daily existence in isolation.
And the eye of the present moment
observes everywhere,
curious, expectant, unsuspecting.

Then, like a Cyclops, the camera
witnesses the unimaginable –
George Floyd calling out
"I can't breathe!"
at the knee of police –
his last breath calling
to his deceased mother.
The sight of it all rocks the city, the nation
out of separation and isolation
into a new consciousness,
as shock waves keep expanding.

The news draws people to the site.
Protestors, ordinary people,
soon take over streets, flood freeway
a veritable stream of humanity
with outcries: "Black Lives Matter!"
Their chants and incantations,
never mind pandemic,
add "No Justice, No Peace."

By night, objects fly through the air
at the fateful site:
Buildings, a police station burn;
businesses are looted;
violent onslaughts threaten life,
neighborhood existence,
peaceful demonstration gone wrong.

National Guard, like Titans,
called out by the governor,
arrive at last, circle demonstrators,
as in a new ritual,
closing in, shrinking the circle,
one protestor by one –
sound of words,
not flash of bullets –
until there were none.
This, as if to say,
yes, there is a better way.
Peace restored in shadow
of billowing fires.

Yet lingering shock waves
of the man's death
go viral, sweep from city to city,
state to state, country to country
with their demonstrations,
like another kind of pandemic.

In coming days, the street where it happened
becomes memorial site. Mourners, protestors

pay their respects with flowers, mementos, signs.
They grieve the loss, uneven status quo –
protestors calling for the world to hear them
calling for long-needed change,
walking and demanding justice,
walking and waiting to be heard.

Season of Construction

And the country opens a bit more,
while pandemic restrictions still remain,
and construction season closes familiar routes.
Released from lockdown,
the once pent-up population
eagerly seeks return to work,
school, leisure activities, bolster economy.
Some continue to work from home.
Businesses operate in reduced capacity,
leaving the unemployed to struggle
to the sound of heavy machinery and trucks.

Demonstrations at the Capitol and other places
flare up with new protests like embers
of a fire that won't extinguish.
Ordinary people assemble, topple statues,
from Christopher Columbus to Robert E. Lee
and more, statues of the historically elevated
and those driven to fight the odds,
now deemed detriment to a better world
by those on the margins. Statues fall
in American cities in desire to repaint,
augment America's image and reality
of what was left out, of missing historical truths
to the chagrin of some, as the world looks on.

And in this construction season,
the street across the drive from where I live,
under construction and blocked off to traffic,

lies torn up as far as the eye can see,
earth's open wound, a cry for healing.
Heavy equipment thunders through the days,
like distant gunfire of an invisible war
carried on within and without.

They Tell Us

Wear a mask.
Wash your hands.
Keep your distance.

Wear a mask.
        Let your eyes do the talking.
Wash your hands.
        Make cleanliness shine.
Keep your distance.
        Stay apart, not out of mind.

Wear a mask
        that eyes find direction.
Wash your hands
        that they can take action
Keep your distance
        that we may lose this pandemic foe.

Wear a mask
        to navigate pandemic's river.
Wash your hands
        to keep yourself and others afloat.
Keep your distance
        to reach the other shore.
We will stand tall together again,
        reconvene our chosen lives in diversity,
                one country full of promise.

What Is Forever?

I

What is forever? Life as we know it?
Shrines and statues left behind?
No, says the poem "Ozymandias."
Only sun and moon and earth
last forever, or so says a story. Really?

What is forever? Do we actually know?
Because we don't live forever, and each
following generation has its own ideas
about that. We only know what went before,
we think, 'til we discover otherwise.

But creation did have its beginning
and not just in the Good Book.

The human way of living,
with its varying expectations, appears fragile
in a pandemic, like soap bubbles
blown into the air, bursting,
not just in one country but in the larger world.

A virus pandemic can upend the system,
politically, socially, emotionally,
economically, financially, strategically.

One unjust killing can question society's
racist tendencies, actually, systemically,
nationally, internationally.

Peaceful demonstrations can escalate
into burning life blood out of a neighborhood,
violently, tragically, unexpectedly.

Toppling of statues questions who deserves
such a pedestal. Statesman or military leader?
Explorer or scientist? Celebrity or athlete?
How about poet or novelist? Artist or architect?
Humanitarian or suffragist? Naturalist or ecologist?
Male or female in diversity? The list is endless.
Life covers new ground, new visions all the time.

II
In this time of pandemic, sultry heat of summer
can hold people down even further.
Unforeseen, thunder and tornado
rumble destructively through landscape.
Wildfires consume forests, wildlife, and homes,
leveling countryside and anything else in its path.

All of this in a string of unbroken events,
expanding demonstrations,
people wearing face masks, social distancing, or not.
Today's system of living may be tip of another pyramid,
become relic of the past sooner than we
imagined for, as yet, unrealized reasons,

while some followers cling, tenaciously,
to the past,

skeptics pursue, ardently,

their own truths,

planners push, incrementally,
into the future,

strategists prepare, prudently,
for the next storm,

scientist work, feverishly,
to develop a Corona vaccine,

and forecasters sketch, guardedly,
an outlook for which there is no vaccine.

We wait, stunned, while the Ace of Change
clamors for adaptation into a new season
of various new directions, as some old roads
already washed out in past and ongoing storms.

Overshadowed

Memorial Day, overshadowed
by pandemic and racial strife,
like the empty beaches at Normandy,
passes without accustomed fanfare and dedication.
Pandemic, though slowed for now,
shows no signs of letting up, dominating
the way people are mandated to live.

Protests over George Floyd's death hold on.
Chaos caused by pandemic restrictions
and wearing of masks lead
to demonstrations at governor's mansion,
as if masks were a politically devised scheme.

Those at a distance, observers,
scientists, medical experts, the elderly,
watch with trepidation, stand guard
to process it all from towers
of their individual isolation. Many carry torch
and banner of a diverse humanity at heart,
silent supporters of the cause,
where "life, liberty, and the pursuit of happiness"
in "one nation under God,
indivisible with liberty and justice for all"
pledge to hold divergent courses.

Zooming In

Three months or more
in social isolation,

hair grows long,
finally free
of round brush and dryer,
curling iron, too.

Even celebrities on Zoom,
have morphed into and share
that at-home look
resembling us ordinary folk.

Yet their images
still surpass ours on Zoom,
since we have not yet mastered
positioning and lighting.

And Zoom, that one-eyed monster, shows us
not the image we imagine
when we look into the mirror,
but a distortion, caricature,
flawed, older version
of ourselves,
as in a carnival's room of mirrors.

Still, we can look in on friends, associates,
who look much like themselves,
in our new world over Zoom,

our new virtual reality,

invited to homes and settings where
we find people at their own comfort levels,
revealing another image
of who they are,
keeping the connection
until we can meet again in person.

Moving Forward in a Pandemic

Pandemic restrictions – and we seek to expand,
clear space in our nest by hand and elbow
in this imposed, solitary life, opportunity knocking.

    The outdated Gateway computer is like
an albatross on the desk, too heavy for me to lift,
too intricate for me to dismantle
in an already overcrowded study,
a suspicious odor emanating from it.

    On my request,
my son soon appears at my doorstep,
social distancing, wearing face mask,
slipping on gloves, a sheepish grin on his face,
saying: "I think this looks bad."

In minutes, he dismantles the equipment
precision of a surgeon,
sets aside usable pieces,
creativity of an inventor,
hauls away the rest,
enthusiasm of a technologist.

    This day closes a relay of time,
when in college days,
I helped his father feed computer cards
into a dinosaur of a free-standing computer.
Eventually, I bought a desk top computer to write
a master's thesis, addicting the writer in me

    to a line of computers to follow
    in the race to update, bringing me
    to my current PC looking for its niche.

    My son clears out the space,
along with the outdated past. He does so
with speed and glee, making it a veritable
Fourth of July celebration for someone eager to update,
and not wanting to be held back
by these otherwise restrictive days.

4th of July

Every year we dedicate the Fourth of July,
Independence Day, to each other,
free spirited as we are, my daughter and I.
The celebration is more than a national tradition;
It has also become our personal tradition.

Today, she arrives with Fourth of July streamers,
wearing a smile that begs a hug,
that we can only motion distantly this year.

This is no less a celebration,
during the pandemic than during normal times,
even if we eat our food at a six-foot distance
outside and using TV trays rather than a table.

We nourish our souls with this shared meal,
drink water of our continuity,
enjoy the ice cream of our chuckles,
exchange trepidations about the virus.

We wonder what may still lie ahead
in a country mixing health concerns,
politics, and protests, as if they were
indivisible parts of one thing
at a time when the country is split.

Outside, on a small table, we set up
the small TV for "The Capitol 4th of July"
virtual celebration and fireworks

in keeping with the day's undaunted spirit.

Two hearts, one country, our bond,
like America's anniversary, is something
to sing about: "Oh say, can you see…?"

Creation

When sun and moon
cradle day and night,

and stars guide
the way,

when clouds and rain
send us inside to reflect,

while lightening
splits horizon,

and thunder
follows after,

then rainbow sends us
into God's atmospheric arms
with wonder,

and grace holds
a steady course.

Our Creation

While pandemic isolation keeps us home,
we seek the path inside
to look at the world outside,
like children who explore and discover
what they did not see before
that will let them move forward again
in the labyrinth of creation
of which we are a part
and which places new challenges before us.

We see life on earth beneath the heavens,
creation of human spirit and actions over eons,
progress and change civilizations
in life and death cycles,
each epoch standing
on shoulders of the previous,
from basic survival of food, shelter, clothing,
from hunting and gathering
to agriculture to science, industry, and technology,
from mountaintop visions to electronic eyes,
ever on.

We move from perception to image,
thought to construction,
cave art to digital image,
hut to skyscraper,
real to virtual,
always from need to purpose to fulfillment,
and on,

as if to unmask the divine,
in a step-by-step approach
that unlocks make-up of nature,
matter, ecosphere, universe,
follows footsteps of discoveries, planned or accidental,
develops process of arts, humanities, and science
from the deep well of humanity's collective spirit and soul.

It's survival of the fittest,
as cultures rise and subside
in the ocean tide of humanity,
of the evolutionary spiral,
where we cling to the life we create.

Between Worlds

Mid-July and four months of social isolation,
the pandemic races on.

Hair grow long now that salons had to close.
It seeks its own natural wave on these hot
and humid days, free of someone's notion
of styling. Staying-home-inspired waves
frame face again, as in younger days.

We carve out time to think, how we,
gregarious humanity, can connect or reconnect
with the world during social isolation, shop
at leisure, find grocery shelves well stocked again,
return to work, meet friends at restaurants,
attend events, get the economy moving again.
In the meantime, it is not enough to write
a check to charity, even when you cannot
be there to help any other way.

Wait. Renewed relationships emerge.
The "How are you?" actually wants to find out
how you are, initiating on both sides
of the phone line. Talking about the old days
and what we are doing now, giving advice
and encouragement, we rediscover each other,
my three brothers and I. The four of us live
each in our own state, as if we needed room
to stretch. We are now brought back to the time
before our parents' passing,

when they were our conduit.

And the friendship of many decades,
that seemed to have changed direction,
the friend who suddenly calls, pours out her heart,
points out the plus and minus of our divergent ways.
It circles back to the beginning
of our college days, when our backgrounds
and situations were so alike in deed and spirit,
they made our friendship converge.
They now become springboard of a new cycle.
And we realize, the choices we make in life
affect others in our circle nearly as much
as they affect us, choices often being more about
immediate needs and circumstances
than they are about disagreements.

It feels good to have hair drape shoulders
in natural waves again,
letting the wind blow through it
without sticky hair spray holding it in place.
Not that it will erase the years nor eliminate
the need for a stylish cut, but it will rekindle
the spirit to embrace the old curiosity
to move forward even into an uncertain future.

A Piece of the Pie

Like the pandemic,
demonstrations move across Twin Cities,
spread across U.S.,
to other countries
with hand-held signs: "Black Lives Matter"
after the terrible death of George Floyd,
leaving some to wonder
how prevalent, how long, how far?
that even other countries mirror the distress.

Let people come together,
sit at the round table of our humanity,
whether black or brown,
indigenous or white,
female or male
and pass the apple pie of community.
There is enough for everyone.
And if there is not,
let's plant more apple trees
in the country's wide-open spaces
of dreams, hopes, and possibilities.

Apple pie tastes best partaken in company,
around the table of sociability and fairness,
where we enjoy rounds of debate and conversation,
discuss problems and solutions,
share the daily purpose,
accept contributions of our cultural gifts,
enjoy diversity of our looks,

compare our troubles and our joys,
reach out a helping hand.
We may discover we are more alike than different
in our quest for daily existence.

America's days are not complete
without the cherished American pie
for everyone, topped
with Liberty, Justice, Equality, and Peace –
because we are all in this life together.

Light Within

Change is our companion,
whom we resist,
as sure as day follows night,
as sure as atmospheric conditions
and weather brush land and sea,
altering face and composition.

Pandemic to demonstrations,
riots to economic setbacks,
it takes body, mind, and spirit
to survive,
move on, seek a new course.

Light within now
guides the way
through fog into the unknown,
detour of the invisible,
construction zones
of separation, isolation, social distance,
staying safe.

The spirit retreats from pandemic
under dome of science,
barely throws lifeline to old ways,
pulls behind half-forgotten memories.
From the street where protests began,
it seeks to design a new map,
lay out new roads,
build new bridges and structures,

design new customs and fashions,
because we are all in this together,

while forging ahead
with our compass
and our steady companion,
change, the eternal pioneer.

Legacy

     News of the congressman's death
reaches the country.
People are saddened, particularly those who looked
for his strong voice in Congress, as he stood up
for truth and justice in this time, where pandemic
and political divisions and contradictions spike.

     News accounts of some of his past ventures air,
almost nostalgically, like his crossing the fateful bridge
marching in peaceful protest in the Civil Rights Movement
of what seems a world away.

     The many eyes of TV cameras take the country,
vicariously, into the virtual reality of his memorial service
to a sort of front-row seat to witness proceedings
and tributes that tell us more about the congressman now
than we discovered during his lifetime.

     He joins annals of history a dedicated leader.
People of all persuasions gather at his farewell service
at Ebenezer church in Atlanta to celebrate the life
and accomplishments of the man they consider
a true American patriot.

     Four past presidents, including both parties
and Speaker of the House, count among the mourners,
eulogizing him, alongside their own lives,
paying tribute to the man and – to American history.

A past president hails the congressman
"founding father of a fairer, better America of tomorrow,"
declaring his journey was not only the past but is ongoing,
stretching into the future and for who knows how long,
as more bridges are crossed.

Inside the church, mourners sit in pews
socially distant, singles, couples, or family groups.
Their responses to speakers enliven sanctuary, while
peaceful crowds, in veritable overflow,
surround the building outside in farewell to a life
peacefully devoted to public service.

In the balance,
the congressman's Voting Rights Bill,
like the ERA, is still waiting to be passed in this
election year. Yet, on the other end, the country's
current president twitters and says,
the nation's upcoming election should be postponed,
because mail-in votes open the door to fraud.

Recipient of the Medal of Freedom,
he wrote to the world:
"Now it is your turn to let freedom ring,"
because true freedom is an equal opportunity employer.
After all, "We hold these truths to be self-evident…"

Seesaw

Pandemic has states on a seesaw
of opening, then pulling back again.
Wearing of facemasks in public places
becomes mandate in Minnesota and other states,
while number of Corona virus cases rise,
and new epicenters of virus outbreaks emerge.

To wear a face mask or
not to wear a face mask,
becomes the question of two camps:
Those who wear masks,
follow social distancing
and those who loudly proclaim their
civil liberties are being violated.

Two camps, two truths:
one logical, the other emotional;
one scientific, the other political;
one of health and survival,
the other of rights at any cost.
Which camp will the virus seek?
As if this were a contest –

Unaffiliated, the virus attaches
to any open host cell, wherever,
whenever, silently, unseen.
Experience taught us
rules of the road and safe driving,
about contagion and prevention.

Who will come to rescue the disbelievers?
Who will survive to tell the story?

How high the numbers today?

Keeping Calm

We count on the spirit
that indomitable essence,
the eternal, varied landscape of the mind
as we live isolated from the world
we once so easily frequented.

It sends us to the inner reaches of imagination,
where we travel free
but not as a bird,
disappearing into clouds
but encapsulated
like a space traveler,
alone,
yet connected
virtually
in conversation on the phone,
in discussion over ZOOM
with those others
in their own capsules,
dressed in their own environments.

They will give you their opinions,
relate stories of neighbors
whom they helped out
in an endless stream
over digits, wires, and waves.

We hold together with thread
pieces of a face mask

that hides real feelings
only the spirit
can unmask, release
on paper or canvas, by instrument
or voice,
share from balconies,
on street corners,
at curbsides
or from homes,
all at a distance,
events we will recall at a later time.

Sundays

"Oh, for a thousand songs to sing,"
Sundays are distinctive days of rest,
change of daily rhythm to rescue
soul and mind from stagnation
in the desert of social isolation.

It was always family day, first
at my parents' house, then
with my own young family,
when we all spent the day together,
at an outing in the park,
a drive to the lake,
a special dinner in the evening,
and – oh yes – dessert.

Now, I still set the day aside, even
in the pandemic, whenever possible.
So, it's streamed church service,
sometimes discussions over Zoom
to invite a new insight or outlook
to recharge the soul.

The day bids something spontaneous,
phone calls with family or friends,
walk around the lake
and contemplation of surrounding trees,
or excursions into creative adventures,
like drawing a haunting image
and truly seeing what I am beholding.

This recharging restores the center,
finds new visions, sharpens the focus,
and leads to new passageways
for the upcoming week's challenges
and directions in a changed world.

Mondays

Mondays are for lining up the week
on a thick notepad, for listing work projects,
appointments, tasks around the house, errands.
The list grows beyond the paper
as the week progresses, even if public events
have already been dropped.

Since the pandemic, Mondays offer
a new start, new plans, new directions,
even if the week's end now proves
there are not enough days in the week
to complete weekly listings.

Working from home allows us to organize,
reorganize, discard what threatened
to crowd us out of our spaces to the point,
where we are never done.

When home doubles as workplace, piles
of projects and notes, rough drafts and sketches,
manuscripts and drawings find their spots
here and there, on sofas, chairs, and tables, until
there is hardly room to sit or place a dinner plate.
Oh, please don't sit there; that colorful paper
is a drawing!

Projects have to be visible when in progress,
like children who need watching.
Once organized, stashed into folders and files,

they disappear. Who will then remind me,
where I filed them among the many folders
created by projects and teaching?

Lessons and presentations are not ready,
until all materials are assembled.
Drawings remain incomplete,
until framed and gracing a wall.
Then the spirit knows where to retrieve them,
and there is enough room to sit again,
for the moment.

Tuesday

She calls
after the dinner hour
to retrospect Sunday
in whose drift
of our meeting
we both still bask.

I thank her
for the antique dish
she had presented me.
She is delighted
I already mended the garment
she had brought with her.

And we set a date
for meeting
week after next
to have a picnic – oh,
near where egrets roost
high up in trees.

Just mother and daughter,
best friends,
on our annual state fair outing
substitute event.

Kitchen Table

Increasingly,
the kitchen table
is birthplace
of poem,
essay,
story,
or anything else
that streams forth,
creeps
from mind's eye,
flows down neck and shoulder,
down arm to hand,
to fingers, onto paper,
sometimes quickly,
sometimes slowly

but steadily,
like headwaters
of the Mississippi,
gathering momentum,
volume,
as they flow south,
dominated
by riverbed
and changes of weather,
flowing,
flowing
into the Gulf of Sensibility.

Section III
Pandemic Campaign: At a Distance

Freedom and Opportunity

Freedom seeks its mark
among a pent-up population, ready to burst
out of emergency restrictions different
in each state, while pandemic rages on
and political conventions seek their venues.

News reports of motorcycle convention
roaring into Sturgis, South Dakota, days ago,
mask-free and without social distancing,
free in the breeze, free in the crowd,
hint of possible super-spreader occasion.

Democratic Convention underway, shifts
to virtual events to avoid spread of virus
with democratic presidential candidate
in declaration of "We the people..."

 It's month and year, 100th anniversary
of women's right to vote, when first woman
of African and East Indian descent,
accepts nomination for vice president
of the United States with the broad smile
of a dream realized for every girl born
in the United States in a sort of a coming of age
of a nation. She proclaims
there is no vaccine for racism,
that there is work to do.

And as the ERA still awaits passage,

the question bears asking, will her model
carry women forward on her shoulders
into the equal opportunity landscape,
past skeptics of different persuasions
in our time and in the future?

Large gathering in Sturgis dissolved days ago,
reports say, sent cases of COVID-19 back
to states from which riders came,
freedom unmasked.

How many infected, did they say?

California Burning

California is burning again,
lightening the flame thrower this time.
Is climate change to blame?

Fire devours woodlands, thousands of acres,
levels homes in its path. People fleeing the blaze
leave behind a life's accumulation and memories,
escape only with bare essentials, as if
from a war zone, where the street stands in flames,
and only embers, ashes, and choking smell
of smoke remain.

Though he resides south of the fire,
I call my brother in Santa Barbara, where he,
transplant from Milwaukee, lives with his wife,
suitcase packed, always ready to evacuate
at moment's notice, which he did countless times.

He and his wife are safe, for now, just dealing
with effects of Corona virus resurgence,
when hair grows long and unruly
and patience to return to a normal life
gets short and strained.

We talk about the usual things,
my sister-in-law's exercise at the pool,
his preference for mystery novels,
my concern over changes in publishing.
"Cultural stuff can be lost in a strict business model

seeking shortcuts to profits," he declares.

We wonder about the twists and turns
the pandemic has on economy, business, schools,
employment, and life in days to come.
Who will go bankrupt or thrive?
How many woodland creatures will survive?
What about the accelerating effects of climate change?

As California smoke dissipates into smoky haze
of Minnesota skies, I hope for a happier reason
to call my brother next time.

Summer's End

Summer is moving into late August,
past a state fair that never was,
like so many events deleted
from the year's calendar
under pandemic clouds,
ignoring the president's outlook
that the virus would be gone by now.

Little remains as usual,
not even the lake across the street,
with flooded grassy shore and dying trees,
not sunrise, nor sunset, which are now deflected in haze
from California's wildfires, mocking clear skies,

nor election campaigns that divide country
in speeches of democracy vs. freedom,
science vs. conspiracy,
hard facts vs. alternate truths,
and just plain differing approaches, showcased
in subdued virtual venues of the democratic candidate
vs. real venues of republican incumbent
firing up his live crowd.

We are startled by the cumulus events
of nearly biblical proportions affecting lives.
Lightening igniting wildfires,
police killings stirring up protests and riots,
hurricanes causing devastation,
pandemic paralyzing people and economy,

politics and voting rights morphing into
country-wide dilemma of various proportions,
all happen in one year's passing.

Solitary days grow long but keep us safe,
working from home, catching up on tasks
and long neglected projects, cleaning out,
discarding what is superfluous, holding course
with what we have. Days grow long,
patience to accept restrictions falls short
as pandemic fatigue sets in.
Perhaps tonight's gentle rain will be our lullaby.

Top of the Hill

  Top of the hill
the bright neighborhood,
   usually quiet,
seems desolate
   since pandemic's start.

  Few cars parked outside,
in driveways,
   on the street weekdays,
almost none Sundays
   that used to team with visitors.
Even patios hold fewer people;
   few voices carry
across the street
   in spontaneous exchange.

  I have not seen my neighbor,
usually out and about,
   in weeks.
Even bird voices seem subdued
   this year.
I miss robin's song in the shrubs,
   mourning dove's coo on the roof.
and the neighbors across
   in casual encounters.

The House Across the Way

    The house across the way,
standing lifeless for weeks
        on the street under construction,
has a new "For Sale" sign
        on the lawn.

    The other Sunday,
dining on the patio,
        we noticed two people
loading furniture onto a pick-up truck
        parked in the driveway.

    On weekdays,
ground shakes,
        air rumbles
with heavy construction machinery,
        closing street
in tandem with pandemic,
        closing life's activities,
isolating the house
        from which dark windows
gape at us across the way.

    Last Sunday,
a car with boat trailer parked
        on cordoned off street
in front of the house,
        garage door wide open,
like the mouth of a hungry whale.

      Days later,
windows come to life in golden glow
      of rebirth, welcoming
two new members and their dog
      to a once empty shell,
joining circle of our community.

School Is Back in Session

      When egrets leave roosts for warmer locales,
schools want to be back in session.

      But in pandemic times, it is all but routine,
intertwined in modern American lifestyle,
economy and politics as it is – American apple pie.

Schools are more than academic institutions.
They are world within world, directed
by rules and regulations contained in the community.
Inside their walls, on athletic fields, in classrooms,
teachers, like parental figures,
guide and offer students views into subject matter
and activities to explore, study, accept
or ignore, in this home away from home,
where students develop mind, body and spirit.
Schools, that meeting place of friends and activities,
help students acquire social values and traditions,
open doors to the future and foster who they are
in the field of dreams, of American identity
to have and to hold for a lifetime.

Since the pandemic, when school is not in session,
society suffers and parents discover
teaching is no child's play,
while students miss teachers, friends, activities.
Employers miss workers. Economy stagnates.
Politicians are left to ponder, juggle the problems.

New ways of teaching are born in this merry-go-round
of education, from distance learning to hybrid
to in-person learning, the latter the preferred model.
But the road now belongs to those juggling the future
with guidelines over student well-being,
safety and effectiveness of learning,
to free parents to make a living, return to work,
to bolster economy, satisfy politics
in this chain reaction of events.

Following pandemic guidelines is no easy task.
Younger students, not ready for such stringent
regimentation, may forget the new rules, unlike
their older, independence-seeking counterparts,
who may find guidelines inconvenient altogether
or interfering with First Amendment rights.
They crowd in high school halls,
college campus gatherings,
convinced they are invincible,
while parents and teachers agonize over safety issues.

Next spring, egrets will return to roost,
raise their young near familiar northland waters.
How will our students fare after storms and stresses
of the past pandemic year, volleying between no school,
in-person instruction, distance learning,
and everything in-between?

Photo Shoot

    In this year of pandemic,
"A family calendar
        is the closest thing
to a family reunion," my brother says.

    He, creator
of an annual picture calendar,
        solicits recent photographs
from siblings residing in different states.

    My side of the family
meets at my house,
        out back, near Colorado blue spruce,
I planted in memory of my dad.

    The tree serves as backdrop
for a spontaneous amateur photo shoot,
        allowing social distancing,
removal of masks.

    It becomes contest for best picture,
between camera and photographer,
        my son and daughter easily winning
with his superior camera,

    their knack for arranging us
in a dance and direction
        of poses and reposes
for just the right shot.

Her long hair needs attention;
his dark glasses get in the way;
　　　and my too relaxed posture,
evokes "oh" and "oh no" and "yes."

　　　We end the wild shoot,
not totally convinced our pictures
　　　will match the glamor shots
sure to find their way into the finished calendar.

　　　Completing the shoot calls
for ice cream cones that now challenge us
　　　not to lose topping of nuts,
between chuckles,
　　　engaging teeth and tongue
to reach the ice cream underneath.

　　　On this summery afternoon,
day before Labor Day,
　　　we linger in our family get-together,
fitting replacement
　　　for the canceled Minnesota Get-Together.

Wildfires on the West Coast

       September arrives fall-like.
Sea gulls fill the air
near lake
as planes fly over
in formation,
commemorate a muted
9/11 celebration
in constrictive pandemic.

Wildfires ignite up West Coast
in regular renewal and growth
of forest lands.
But fanned
by drought and winds
and climate change, they rage,
devour homes, devastate lives
in their path,
adding stress
to protests and pandemic.

Call to my middle brother
in Oregon confirms his safety
and that of his family
for now,
fires at least twenty miles away.
"There are tornadoes
in Minnesota," he says.

But they seem nothing like fires

I saw move along in the news
of West Coast areas,
sky glowing red
by day and by night,
unless choked out
by dark, billowing smoke.

      Winds should die down
over the weekend,
weather report says.

Wildfires Moving North

In the dark eastern,
early morning sky,
sliver moon
shadows Venus,
second planet from the sun.

At sunrise,
an orange sun
fans out.
Cloud-like haze
disguises Minnesota sky

with its offshoot
of western wildfires
that keep burning
California to Oregon,
to Washington and Canada.

We watch the news
in dread
and trepidation
fires and smoke plumes
fire gods created,
and climate change
humans have wrought.

The Chase

Staying healthy in pandemic times
means staying home, except for essentials
which seem to grow in number each day.

Mind turns to paper and pencil,
keyboard and computer,
goes on excursions
without enough words,
as they slip away in the storm,
disappear into folder, drawer, haze of the day,
Zoom meeting, telephone conversation
without spontaneity of face-to-face exchange
to keep up with changing language.

Even the doctor's office searches for words,
asking if I can remember three in a row,
"leader," ah yes, one who
keeps the country safe
in all ah, "seasons,"
at the round, ah, "table" of exchange.
Drawing of candidates raises chuckles,
connotation hiding
in the word, oh, ah – "caricatures."

But who can survive this distancing
without haze of mind, oh, ah – the "stoic?"
especially when haze of sky
is no fog. It's the smoke out West
that causes the problem of memory

like pandemic, fire, hurricane – disasters
of, oh, ah – "biblical proportions,"
demonstrations looking for the right
oh, ah – "vocabulary," Black Lives Matter,
rounding the five-in-one challenge
of this election year.

Excursions stop at the poem,
secret gold mine of words
that slip into consciousness, stir memory,
before they become hazy again, and insights disappear,
washing away in the swollen river of current events.

Waiting for Change

Autumnal equinox
and 200.000 lives are lost
to the pandemic, regardless of ethnicity,
race, religion, or political affiliation,
as we struggle on.

Meanwhile, Minnesota firefighters
help out in Oregon,
and a Black woman's death
is still being investigated in New York,
while hurricane and tropical storm
devastate countryside,
and we mourn
Supreme Court Justice's passing
on Rosh Hashana,
while the economy struggles,
and the presidential campaign wrangles
its way forward

We look on as in a dream,
where nothing seems the way it was
or should be or what we hoped for,
in a kind of unreality.
Our lives changed into capsule existence;
bright blue skies transformed
into a greyish haze;
Zoom meetings see our way
through isolation

Evelyn D. Klein

into discussions
as if we existed on separate planets.
We wait endlessly
for the election to be final,
for the pandemic to be over,
and for a miracle or leader to help us move forward
to a more natural, equitable, freer,
economically stable existence.

Construction Season Ending

      Sun rises pink,
greets a hazy horizon
over quiet neighborhood lake
this fall day.

Construction season
still cuts through the atmosphere
to the chagrin of nearby residents,
work in progress
on a drain field claiming the meadow
across the street.

Construction trucks barrel
down footpath like mammoths
ready to feed their young
but delivering sod and plantings
to cover the wounded earth
so near the lake.

Perhaps later is a better time
for a walk around this now birdless lake
to see tall grass and wildflowers
weave in the breeze,
check out trees like old friends,
some of whom now stand bare,
their branches extended skyward,
as if to implore the heavens.

At sunset tonight,
visible from lake's southern edge,
the increasing moon will appear
just below Jupiter and Saturn.

The Neighbor

My neighbor across the street,
    with whom I'm used to visiting,
is mostly invisible
    since the pandemic.
Her garage door, facing mine,
    remains closed.

With social distancing,
    her hearing loss,
it's difficult to communicate.
    So, on occasion
and with a smile,
    as words float away
in the wind,
    we wave to each other,

like the potted
    red and pink geraniums,
waving in the wind,
    those she admired
under my window
    wave across the street
to her red and white geraniums
    at the end of the sidewalk
wave like old friends
    who do not need words
for their connection.

Changing Season

      She calls. We set up
second of October for our outing,
last day of her vacation.
We meet for a picnic lunch
in my yard, socially distancing
with chicken salad croissants,
berries for dessert.

      We reconnect from time to time,
when we talk recipes
in-person or over the phone,
discussing foods she used to enjoy
at home as a child
or at my table as an adult,
mother to daughter.

      Other times, she guides me
through straights of technology,
access to Skype or internet
requirements that send me
out to sea. She guides me
patience of an angel,
in a reversal of roles,
daughter to mother.

      Just last Monday,
we coordinated our shopping trip
to a clothing store like a team,
in a give-and-take of opinions

strengthening dimensions
of our relationship,
woman to woman.

     Today, we walk around the lake
like old friends,
warmth of sun in our faces,
briskness of fall air in our nostrils,
crunch of leaves under foot.
We chat with and pass a neighbor,
keeping our distance.
My daughter spots geese resting
on rocks near shore, points out
a caterpillar inching across path.
I remark on the everchanging,
leafless willow trees extending
limbs near and across the water.
We contemplate apple trees
and reach for their red-cheeked fruit,
examine and compare our treasures.

     At the end of the path, we inspect
the nearly finished drain field
extending from street to lake,
evidence of life's unfaltering progress

     Having completed our circle
around the lake,
we motion our distant hugs
to each other in parting,
our relationship moving forward

like seasons of the park,
in the mutual bond
that social distancing cannot undo.

October Day

    This balmy, early October day,
I crunch through the park's
        fallen leaves in the fall of my days.

    Two boys side by side
pass me on the path, and a boy
        and his grandmother on their bikes
pass me in the other direction,
        calling out: "To the left!"

    The lake sparkles diamonds
in the sunshine, where on or near
        center island of rocks, geese and ducks
and two gulls quietly converge,

    like thoughts of three books out
looking for publishers, they wait
        in season of harvest and migration,
while two crows caw overhead.

    On the other side of the path
in a still green tree, a multitude
        of different bird voices chirp and tweet
in chorus of lively assembly,

    like the multitude of thoughts
cruising in mind, pressing for release
        on the page, not Ivy League thoughts
nor Hollywood celebrity puns but plain

    Midwestern, harvested, everyday thoughts.

    As I round the corner
to the street where I live,
    sunshine nearly blinds, slows my pace.
I draw in its energy, propelling forward,
    always forward, step by step
on a glorious day like this.

Reconnect

This October day, I call my long-time chum
of Milwaukee college days, when we saw the world
from the same slant, to say: "Happy birthday!"
but have to leave a message instead.
When she calls back, we chat and chat –

like we used to a long time ago
when we first reconnected in the Twin Cities
on separate tracks, having stood up
for each other's weddings.
We regularly talked on the phone then,
while she taught school,
and I was a stay-at-home mom.
We came to dinner at each other's home.
On the phone, we shared the process of sewing
a life's wardrobe, all the while
she grew a garden into a small park,
and I eventually built a new life
around teaching and writing –

We are as different as earth and sky but
affected by similar youthful experiences and hopes.
In time, our lives took different directions,
she in perspective of gardener
and I in reflection of writer and teacher
in the chosen community where we live.
The pandemic brought us together again.
We now chat in a volley, just as we once did.

We reconnect on the basis of old bonds.
She and her husband now rake leaves for their garden
while I gather pages of writing into a collection.
We chat about election, health and education,
merits and dangers of eating out during a pandemic.

Our talks trail on, and it seems an hour on the phone
is not enough to catch up in the continued reconnect,
grown from seedlings of long ago and our link
between earth and sky, artists, each in our own Eden.

Vote for Your Life

On the screen it says:
"Vote for your life."
Mostly, I run for my life
to perk up the spirit,
exercise the heart –
for that sense
of energy and freedom.

One hundred years ago,
women did vote
for their lives,
to be heard,
not just to be seen.

I vote
for family and friends,
for colleagues and readers,
neighborhood and community,
and for the country.

You feel part of the whole,
when you vote,
whether your voice
is a name or a no-name.
Sometimes
the chosen candidate wins.

What does one vote
really matter, you may ask,

or even many votes,
when Electors, not voters,
decide the outcome?
But what if voting is
a privilege
and civic responsibility
to be revered and exercised
in a democracy?

A Rushing of Clouds

Popcorn clouds
rush across sky from the northwest,
as if on some urgent errand,
obscuring sun
only now and then
in their push to move on.

Robins flutter excitedly
in cluster of trees near lake shore,
in silence
of their concealed gathering.

Geese float quietly
on lake waters close to shore,
like the fallen leaves
carried along by current,
before migration.

The tree still in full plumage,
teaming with chorus
of bright bird voices the other day,
is eerily quiet today.

On my jaunt around the lake,
I stop by the bench
where my daughter and I rested
last Sunday,
on one of the fleeting warm
autumn days,

and contemplate
the peaceful scene shore to shore
that may find its way
onto a book cover drawing.

Native Peoples Day

October painted trees
deepest red to rust,
orange to brightest yellow,
this Columbus Day or
newly coined,
Native Peoples Day.

Wind tosses tree crowns
as people gather
at the newly renamed lake
Bde Maka Ska
in Minneapolis,
not for a ghost dance
but for a march,
a sign reading:
"I'm proud to be Ojibway."

Wind stirs up
fallen leaves,
as people march
into consciousness
that a statue of Christopher Columbus
can have two sides,
two interpretations,
two ways of living,
leaning in opposite directions.
And a heartbeat re-emerges
seeking a new 21st century direction,
seeking a united spirit,

as the statue begins to topple.

Cloud Watching

Tufts of clouds,
light grey
with gold or pink edges,
move east across
deep azure blue sky.

Intermittently, large
dark grey clouds
cover sun
in a game
of hide-and-seek,
at times releasing showers.

Like the endlessly
traveling clouds,
few things ever
remain completely
the same,

not the rising and falling,
rising and falling
Covid clouds,
infections and deaths
crossing
from state to state.

Old Friends

    These fall days,
the lawn is covered
with fallen leaves,
shades of rust to gold.

    Inside, African violets
stretch along window,
a palette of colors
from purple to white,
pink to blue,
and shades in-between
of another bloom,
despite waning daylight.

    Some are gifts of friends
from long ago; others are new.
I study the variations among them,
similarities and differences
just like in people. They are all
from the family of violets,
yet no two are the same
in blossom or leaf,
color or shape,
unless they are from the same plant
which you can propagate
from a leaf cutting.
I like to meditate
over their personalities
that light up my days

and rooms of my house,
carry on an unspoken conversation
with them in sight, thought, and touch.

African violets rescue me
from pandemic isolation
with their radiance
and blossom memories
like loyal, long-time friends.

Pandemic Fatigue

Overcast skies,
brisk, cold winds,
frost at night,
rain and snow by day,
the river pulsates over the unseen.

No more outside dining.
Time to move back indoors,
where it is warm,
to life as it used to be,
celebrate birthdays,
weddings,
prepare for the holidays,
go back to work,
to school,
open economy,
mingle with friends
just as always.

You are remiss
if you can't explain
your high risk in a pandemic
to those in denial
and simply shelter at home.
You are not welcome
at the party,
even if it is planned for outdoors,
if you are the only one
wearing a face mask

when they gather without.

Skies are overcast.
Experts warn
cases are rising
in most states.
But what do they know
in this political year
of wishful thinking,
while the river pulsates over the unseen.

Gone Virtual

For years
we watched imagination
cross the screen
in Hollywood,
followed news around the globe
on television.

Now we travel
digital Pegasus
through dark valleys
of ghouls
up bright hills
of virtual reality.

On Zoom we visit family,
meet friends,
attend meetings,
conduct business,
consult physicians,
even though it's way past 1984.

Not sun or rain,
sleet or snow,
nor October snowstorm
can prevent us from getting through
with Pegasus, that updated router,
to take us to our destination.

Moving Forward

Like a fortress,
Saint Paul's Cathedral
presides on the hill
over neighborhood, city, landscape,
and river.

Like the fortress
that is God,
the spirit travels river of life,
scouting, exploring souls
of generations.

New ages of living,
being
examine the depths
of change
in a pandemic,
survey an outlook
of people
trying to move
forward
in stalwart of the past,
in current
of the present,
not aware
of what lies
beneath
the surface
of the pulsing

waters
but slowly moving,
moving
forward.

Section IV
From Elections through Holidays: Staying Safe

Haunted

To carry on a conversation,
whether in company,
solitude, pandemic, or isolation,
requires paper, lots of paper
in case of computer malfunction,
or printer unavailability
tech chat misfiring,
or simple paper preference.

I can think it over
without interruption,
keep my train of thought in-takt
or go off on suddenly inspired excursions,
before I spring these thoughts on reader or listener,
even if they are never cast in stone.

My discourse with the world,
spontaneous and involved,
may not be what it wants to hear
or the way I put it.
But I have to convey it,
because some may want to listen
after all, and
because I need to solve the puzzle,
figure out and clear up
these haunting thoughts
which frequent my mind
to make sense of the world
in which I live.

This accounts for my continued staring contest,
alternatingly,
with paper and computer.

The Discourse

          The written word,
oh, the written word,
it can give us away, or
it can give credibility to what we say.
It can keep us on the straight and narrow
that we won't lose our way
in underbrush of a busy life,
or electronic excursions full of variable print.
          The written word can lessen the load.

          The written word allows us
to go back to what was said or written just then,
allows us to check pages of history
for what was or may have been
and trace events forward to today,
where we can pick up the trail
          to extend into the not yet.

          Pictures,
oh, pictures,
the written word begs for pictures to illuminate
the abstract, the unspoken, shine light
on what we say, read, or write,
in case words missed something,
because the world is round,
and sun lights day and moon lights night,
so we can see our version of the environs
in different shades, shadows, and darkness.
Pictures bring to life words in their sentences,

    the inner view brought outside.

    Pictures add their own story
with their shades of light and dark
in non-verbal expression, expanding the vision.
Pictures furnish the missing link, form the whole,
giving us more words to carry on the discourse,
    to carry on the discourse.

Birthday Shopping

      My daughter and I meet
to spend time together,
but wearing masks,
birthday shopping for new shoes,
struggling with social distancing.

      At the store,
we find shelves after shelves
lined with sandals, heels, stilettos,
fashion dictates,
all lonely for lack of attention.
The few customers present eye shoes
you can walk in,
keep warm in.
My daughter looks for navy,
so popular, yet rarely displayed.
At last, she finds flats
that show off foot and ankle
but provide solid footing.

      We agree,
    stilettos captivate when a woman lets
    her legs drape,
    seated high on a chair,
    and the camera's lense
    catches them just so,
    like some political rallies
    or promises that fill the air
    with a future that may or may not stand up.

Today's woman knows she needs shoes
to walk solid ground,
where her voice is heard
when she stands in line to vote.
A woman is not just a picture,
even if her Mona Lisa smile enchants,
but a pioneer of spirit and deed
to stand alongside her man.

This year, wind howling,
Halloween's blue moon
will light up the night.
The election will tread on its heels
three days later.
And in this whirlwind time of pandemic,
masks and social distancing,
my daughter's birthday celebration,
not to be preempted,
will follow mid-month
in a newly fitting family configuration.

Fall Campaign

      Trees have shed
remaining leaves
after the early snowfall
that has nearly melted again,
just before Halloween.
Squirrel's nests loom
exposed in tree crooks.
Crabapple trees show off red fruit
on bare branches.
Carved pumpkins decorate doorsteps.

      All the while,
election campaign resounds
in bursts of energy
in a place
between past and future,
volleying between messages,
the incumbent's "Corona, corona, corona…
We are rounding the corner,"
or "Four more years,"
and the other candidate's
"Before we can fix the economy,
we need to control the virus"
and setting course for
"a more inclusive America."

And we lean back
in our spectator seats,
wary of pandemic's reach

and conflicting messages
but knowing our goal
is to stay safe,
yet all the while wondering whether
our voices will be heard
when mail-in ballots are counted.

Halloween Ghosts

In the eastern sky,
blue moon evades clouds,
makes lake waters glow.

Wind howls unceasingly,
sweeping leaves across lawn and empty street,
the night seemingly alive
with spirits like the times
when the children were little
and went trick or treating with their dad,
and the streets were teaming
with like-minded ghosts and goblins.

Wind keeps rattling the house,
reminiscent of times children came to the door,
and I dispensed candies,
or later, when my young students
came to the door,
giving themselves away,
blurting out German words and phrases
learned at school.

Something keeps bumping the house.
On the west side, the window is bright,
drawn with moving shadows.
Getting out of bed,
I peer through the blinds.
It is bright, suddenly calm,
not a soul afoot.

Wind groans again,
as I return to bed.
No one came to the door tonight,
the spirit keeping us inside
in this drawn pandemic,
where we seek strength within,
where the God of our being
keeps us
in the most difficult
and ghostly of times,
day before All Saints Day.

Geraniums

    Potted geraniums
brought into the garage
    to protect from October's frost
make their way back
    into November's yard.

    One more week
of warm weather
    will keep them
to enjoy the welcome smile
    they send
like from an old friend
    each time I return home
from walk or errand.

Roses and Books

Another load of poetry books
arrives in the garage,
delivered by the publisher,
right next to the potted roses,
placed in the box,
brought inside to winter.

    The box is still open
as blossoms still come forth.
Once they open,
I will cut them
to place into a ready vase.

    The fascination of roses
is like the anticipated elections.
Buds are anxiously awaited
but thorned stems might prick
like events of campaigns
and concerns over outcome.

    Against the odds, the roses
will survive another winter in the garage.
Staying safe at home,
so will we survive pandemic.
When roses will sprout and bloom again
next year, they will celebrate
moments of our renewed being.

Books, too, will bide their time,

lose their anonymity,
when the cycle of readings, events,
returns to celebrate stages of growth.

Autumn's Hub

      Waning warm days
make lake hub
of bird life again,
ducks swimming
in small groups,
geese claiming rock island
in lake's center,
swans surrounding them
with their whiteness,
gulls circling above
with their cries
      in autumnal practice.

      Here is room for each
in season's hush
of peaceful coexistence,
      flocks drawn to sun and water.

      I am just one small part
of that
on solid ground, though,
where I stand alone,
drawing, observing, writing,
before I return to the every-day,
where I float on the edge,
for I can only be
who I am,
a living being,
child of nature,

human nature,
thinking, anticipating, dreaming,
    like the birds, like the birds…

Moving On

    Balmy days of autumn,
curtain of leaves having fallen,
       trees show off
startling configurations of branches
       as if in some inviting dance.
Geese and gulls, ducks and swans
       dot lake, line shoreline
in peaceful assembly.

    Election winds blow
in a race between past and future,
       with promise and hope
of honor and integrity,
       freedom and democracy,
the common good
       to bring together
differing mindsets,
       one America moving on,
because we are all Americans.

    Fallen leaves protect roots and soil.
Collaboration and inclusion,
       protect the heart and soul of a country,
guard lives of citizens
       from pandemic,
preserve liberty of a people
       to voice who they are,
champion pursuit of happiness, the dream.

      People are dancing in the streets
with din and horns of approval
      at the election results.
Controversy stirs behind the scenes
      like passing clouds above.
Both parties having voted in record numbers.
      A new president-elect and vice president-elect,
first woman ever, carry the day with votes, electors
      after the seesaw of 2020 campaigning.
The opposition stands in disbelief.

      Juncos on the ground
foreshadow colder weather.
      Geese in noisy assembly
rehearse flying formation,
      one goose at point, the rest falling in line
for the perfect kite formation,
      while stragglers struggle to catch up,
because it takes the whole flock
      to create the aerodynamics
of their joint journey south.

November Maneuvers

November sky resounds
cackling of geese,
three separate bands flying
with stragglers here and there.
It is late in the season
for geese to keep maneuvering like that.
But lake waters are still open.

Like the birds,
people traversing lake
are split into factions,
those wanting the country to stay open,
grappling over pandemic conspiracy,
their right to choose,
vs. those following emergency mandates,
scientific guidelines
with masks and social distancing.

It takes one bird's
experience and strength to fly point,
for the rest to fall in line,
kite formation, behind it
that they will manage together
the arduous flight
to winter habitat,
so they can return in spring
to nest and thrive once again.

What will it take for citizens to unite

behind a new lead
to winter the surge,
beat the virus' blow
with vaccinations and Covid relief
that will ensure renewal
of life, liberty, country, and outlook,
so all can return to summers
of their content?

Thanksgiving 2020

Thanksgiving 2020 is like no other.
We consider blessings that grace days
with walks in nature,
while home holds the course,
and chores keep us connected to life's flow.

We are thankful
for essential workers in grocery stores,
in medical facilities,
in scientific laboratories,
in factories, and more.

We appreciate
discovering or rediscovering
ways to connect with the world
through phone conversations,
e-mails, or across the way greetings,
not to forget donations to the food banks.

I am grateful
for adult children who find new ways
to connect, delivering an evergreen basket.
They initiate our visit over Skype
that brings us, like pilgrims,
to a new continent,
so we can share thoughts and news,
enjoy a virtual tour of the son's new home
that lets us share in his joy.

I am blessed
with the view from my sunroom window
lined with African violets that are still blooming,
looking outside onto blue spruce
and crabapple tree
that chickadees like to inhabit year-round.

I am thankful for the fireplace,
pen and paper in hand, a cup of hot tea nearby,
wearing comfortable slippers,
allowing me to reflect over flickering flames
on these solitary days.

Black Friday

At dusk,
over roof tops
and through bare branches
of linden tree,
nearly full moon
appears picture perfect
in frame of my study window,
impervious to pandemic,
filling me with amazement.

A Gathering

Never before have I seen
so many geese gather
on a partially frozen
Minnesota lake in December.
They line up around the oval
of still open water
in the lake's center,
where a few geese swim,
two gulls circling overhead,
their voices muted,
as if in communal prayer,
part of some holy ritual.

At the shore,
majestic tree clusters
reach heavy branches skyward
as if in adoration.
Bird voices chirp and tweet
in full chorus in the thicket.

From the water,
wings unfolding,
geese rise in bands
into the air
over roof tops and tree crowns,
their voices trailing
as they fly west, following
the late afternoon sun.

Inspiration

During this pandemic,
Zoom has become
our refuge,
our meeting place,
the next best thing
to being there,
to hold on
to what or who
is needed,
to what or who
is dear,
while we wait
for magic
of science
to rescue us
from ourselves
and the virus.

Nine Pandemic Ways of Thinking

The lockdown turns home into a fortress,
with only virtual admittance, where we rule.

Essentials allow us access to the once public domain
for the sake of food, healthcare needs, maintenance.

We wash hands of the virus, like of our world,
family, friends and every outside activity and more.

Face masks accord stylish new accessories,
insuring our mystique in public places.

Social distancing introduces a new dance,
three side steps meaning I do, no steps I don't.

Elbow bump tempts our connection, replacing
handshake in the dance's whirlabout maneuver.

Large gatherings celebrate super spreader events
among the entitled, the believers, the fun seekers.

Covid-19 does not discriminate between parties, religions;
it just circulates between countries and mutates.

Vaccine to the rescue, can open the country again,
but not minds of disbelievers, doubters, and skeptics.

The Train of 2020

The 2020 train, with its wagon loads,
barrels steadily toward the holidays
on tracks of pandemic and fear, sparks
of deceit threatening to ignite landscape.

Flood of pandemic rises precariously,
while health care workers
struggle to do their best to heal the sick,
Minnesota holding its own for now.

The president-elect, ready and awaiting
Inauguration Day in the new year,
lines up his cabinet for confirmation hearings
without traditional alignment.

The incumbent, surprised and doubting
the lost election, contends it stolen,
something no judge
or court can seem to verify.

Demonstrators, desperate
and demanding lifting of restrictions,
want restaurants and small businesses to reopen,
despite pandemic's rise.

Powers that be, concerned and planning
to return the young to in-person learning at school,
draw mixed reactions
from educators and from parents.

And the train races on in smog of events,
haze of outcomes, speeds
toward a vaccine, another stimulus package,
reenergizing of economy
over bridge across river of division.

It rumbles through tunnel of time and uncertainty,
eager to unload what is true, discard what is twisted,
save health of a people, then coasting
toward dawn of new promise, convergence of its travelers,
coasting on tracks of their uncommon history.

Advent Reflections

Difficult times
like these
have us hold on
to the light
of Christmas,
alone or in a crowd,
with family or a friend,
with those in need.
We hold on
to bridge the divide,
in thought or deed,
virtually or actually,
in rain or snow or sunshine,
in moonlight,
wishing upon a star,
sitting by the fireplace
of remembrance and anticipation
in song, picture, or prayer.
We hold on
to reflections of Christmas
in mirror of its past,
birthplace of new tomorrows,
truth of our convictions,
faith in our tomorrows,
holding on
to the light,
holding on,
holding on.

Christmas Eve Light

While Christmas lights sparkle
in many neighborhoods,
Saturn and Jupiter, in Christmas star mode,
guide us to Christmas and church services,
streamed from churches,
many left with empty pews,
celebrating the Birth. Yet
a Minnesota blizzard, like the pandemic,
threatens to obscure the way for those
wanting to go home for Christmas.

It's the year of virtual or distance
Christmas Eve services. The church
welcomes onlookers with lighted trees
at its portals but leading into an empty sanctuary.
Inside, the camera shows lights near the altar,
and poinsettia plants gently reflect the season.
Sweet music of Christmas, choir of Angels
celebrate, discreetly, draw the spirit
into the holy with their promise.
Readings and prayers uphold
remembrance of Christmas past
within stark walls of this celebration.
Stained glass windows add their story.
All the while, candles flutter, light sanctuary.

Lighted Christmas candles
pack church's center aisle
side to side, end to end,

Evelyn D. Klein

clear to the exit doors,
a flowing river of light,
flowing past row after row of pews
empty of living souls.
We witness in wonder,
as if in remembrance
and prayer of those lost,
lost since church's inception,
lost in growing pandemic,
where the future appears
less about Birth
and more about Resurrection.

Christmas Day

Sunlight
brightens
Christmas Day.
This small family converges,
anxiously greeting each other
at the long-awaited gathering,
as in a reprieve of spirit.
Wearing masks to match outfits,
as if attending a costume ball, we gather
not around the tree, as we usually do,
but in three separate stations around the room
to accommodate distancing,
like in an outlandish new ritual.
No need for an elaborate meal
to warm renewal of our bond,
when our unity nourishes
and the wine of sharing flows
in our veins. Socially distant interactions
become a game of charades.
Opening of gifts becomes
another form of communication,
an exchange of life's practical side
with warmth of winter coats,
practicality of tools,
efficiency of paper pads,
finishing touch of sweet treats,
gifts wrapped creatively to extend suspense,
all in acknowledgement of who we each are.
We share this short time,

as if it were a live,
on-stage appearance
of an annual presentation,
until curtain fall –
Then each of us,
with gestured hugs,
retreats backstage
into our individual
world of reality.

Year's End

      New Year's Eve,
that glittery, noisy time of year
      of laughter and singing
ordinarily celebrated
      with parties and dancing,
has a subdued tone this year.

      New Year's Eve without parties
does not seem a celebration
      as people hunker down
in small gatherings
      or no gatherings at all.

      You can watch televised programs
in safety of your living space, instead,
      but without the joy and excitement.
You can watch the ball drop
      in New York Square on the tube,
but without antics and interviews of the crowd.

      Or you can watch
Fred Astaire and Ginger Rogers
      glide across the screen
in their classic dance moves
      through romance and events
of their carefree films,
      recapturing spirit of past new Year's Eves,

      until step and spin of it all

carry you back to New Year's dances
      with that one person in your life,
stepping, turning in illusion,
      dream flair of ballroom dancing,
drifting off in tender arms of sleep
      well before the midnight hour,
spinning into the who knows what
      of the new year.

Promise

We keep our eyes on our city, our country
as its protagonists move in closer to us
during this isolation, this anonymity.
We watch, follow events, chaos,
voices of diffusion
from pandemic to natural disasters,
demonstrations to political events.
We, members of the neighborhood,
the village that is our country,
cast our days together
with the neighbors we want to protect
while staying safe ourselves.
Our country is imprint of humanity's family,
where diversity denotes strength, beauty, progress.
No differences, no fears are so great
they cannot join
the round table of truth and promise,
where liberty and justice,
the pursuit of happiness,
good health for all
can find their place of continuity and growth
under the People's Dome of Democracy,
dwelling place of the American Dream.
For this land was made for you and me.

Quarantine Companions

Lockdown. Quarantine.
Alone. We are all in this pandemic together.
It's isolation. Isolation.

> We work our way through shadowy forest
> of Covid, through thickening, rising brush.

At home, houseplants become companions
who beg attention, conversation.
It's a good time for annual transplanting,
so African violets can carry forward their colors,
each begging its own name
to go with that personality.

> And the Covid curve rises and falls, rises and falls
> as we trudge through the woods without path.

Let's transplant the white violets,
for each person who died but not from Corona,
those succumbing to illness,
freedom fighter Congressman,
the Woman Supreme Court Justice,
and the ones whose lives were taken
by those meant to protect,
the man who died on the street,
the woman who died in her home.

Let's transplant light blue violet
for the scientists entrusted to find a cure,

a vaccine to stamp out Corona.
Let's transplant the double purple for healthcare people,
the purple with white rim for essential workers,
the single purple for firefighters.

Let's transplant the pink violet
for the new Woman Supreme Court Justice,
the rose-colored violets
for the candidates on either side running for president,
the ice pink for the incumbent,
the maroon for the woman, first woman of color,
nominated for vice president,
the violet color one for the man nominated,
by the opposing party, for president
who promises to bring the country together.

So many violets crowding in one space,
so many souls lost alone
and not enough violets stacked
along this window wall, whose sheltering blinds
let through light but not direct sun,
too many to count,
all like children looking for promise.

> Surely the woods are too shadowy for violets,
> so home is a good place to stay safe.

Transplanting hands can dig deep into soil
to connect with mother earth,
until skin's furrows and nails turn black
and require thorough scrubbing like those

of health care workers or ordinary people
washing off contagion.

      We struggle through the woods, and hope
      not to trip looking for the clearing,
              looking, looking.

Now to remember
not to water violets too much,
avoid direct sunlight
no matter how much it goes against the grain,
shelter them behind blinds
but take time to linger over them,
extol their diversity,
engage in conversation with them,
to ensure all will thrive in new organic soil,
not to develop as they were
but as they are going to be
in the new period of growth,
in the period of new growth.